HAPPY TO MEET ME

Guided Self-Discovery Journal
For Self-Love and Happiness

Calista J. McBride

This Journal Belongs to

_____

_____

Table of Contents

A Gift and an Invitation

As a way of saying thanks for your purchase, I'm offering a **Free Bonus** *14-day Self-love Challenge* handbook exclusively for our readers.

With this companion handbook, you'll discover the best ways to naturally boost your self-love on a daily basis.

Simply send an email to calistamcbride@gmail.com
Title the email *"More Self-love"*

As you go through this journal, you might find yourself wondering where to find more journals or books like this.

What if I told you that you could get them for **free** and **exclusively before release**?

If you're interested, I'd like to invite you to join our Happy Community.

Simply send an email to calistamcbride@gmail.com
Title the email *"Happy Reads"*

Happy reading

"Who looks outside, dreams; who looks inside, awakes."

– *Carl Gustav Jung*

Introduction

Life's an endless journey of self-exploration. Just when you thought you figured out one aspect, a new challenge comes your way. From an early age, society has told you who you should "be" and how to "behave", but what really defines you?

A huge struggle that many people have is they simply do not like themselves, whether they hate the body they have or they dislike their personality and lack confidence.

Journaling is the ultimate catalyst for change. It provides a way for you to find a new perspective in your life. When you can shift your views, the thoughts and feelings you have, everything becomes easier.

Successful influencers, like Oprah Winfrey, Ellen DeGeneres, Tony Robbins, and many more, have created great lives because of their daily journals. Look, this journal is not about making you write every day. It's about helping you discover healthy thoughts that enable you to create the life you love.

This journal is about finding yourself. It's time to cultivate self-love, so you actually enjoy the person that you spend the most time with. No one else can convince you to love yourself. It is a fulfillment you will explore on your own. If you want better relationships, abundance, health (mind and body), and everything you've ever dreamed of, you can achieve it.

It's time to change, and that starts by looking inward.

Chapter One: How to Use This Journal

This writing prompts journal for self-discovery will enable you to be in harmony with yourself, build personal empowerment, and create new insights that can help carry you to an entirely new life.

They are not just randomly designed prompts - they are placed specifically. These prompts will stimulate you to provide deep insights. They are meticulously crafted and placed to offer new and exciting ideas.

You can naturally improve your life for the better, with as few as five minutes addressing these prompts for daily reflection.

One thing that can help you through this writing prompts journal for self-discovery is to pinpoint a few feelings or thoughts or other main themes for you to overcome.

I will provide you with daily writing prompts and guidelines, but having a few goals of your own can help.

As you work through this journal, you will discover that it becomes easier to remain positive and happy. You will learn to love yourself more and remain compassionate towards who you are.

Roadmap

This is an undated journal, which means you can begin at any time that is comfortable for you.

Keep in mind the point is to have fun. There is no "right" answer, and it's not possible to make mistakes. This is a learning process, which means sometimes a mistake is going to be more valuable than learning the lesson. Also, curiosity should always come before anything else.

It's OK to get messy. Capture your real voice and be honest because no one else is going to hold you to your own word. **It's your journal**.

The beginning will be all about **self-awareness**. You can't heal and grow unless you become highly aware of your limiting perspective of the world and the roadblocks keeping you from the life you deserve.

The next section is about **self-love.** It's going to help you realize your worth and become aware of the things you enjoy about others.

Then we will focus on **self-esteem**. As you become more aware of how you move through the world and begin the journey to loving yourself, now it's time to elevate your sense of self-worth.

A Promise to Yourself

Before getting started, it is time to write a promise to yourself. Write your most compelling reasons below. You can go back to these whenever you feel like you need more inspiration or motivation to keep moving forward.

Ask yourself a few questions before getting started if you're having trouble finding your reasons:

- What are the most compelling reasons for using this journal now?

- How will it impact the quality of your life and the people you care about?

- What are you hoping to gain that will make you feel fulfilled?

Fill in the blank now.

I am journaling because I want to:

Chapter Two: Self-discovery writing prompts

Remember, it's undated, so you can go at your own pace. Without further ado, let's begin.

Self-discovery writing prompts: Raising Self-Awareness

"Everyone sees what you appear to be, few experience what you really are."
— *Niccolò Machiavelli*

1. Common Misconceptions
What do other people fail to see in you? What is one thing about you that you wish everyone else automatically knew?

"Reading is to the mind what exercise is to the body and prayer is to the soul. We become the books we read." — *Hal Elrod*

2. Clear and undeniable

What is natural about you? Whether it is the way you look, the way you act, the way you feel. You are natural because…

"I imagine that the intelligent people are the ones so intelligent that they don't even need or want to look 'intelligent' anymore."
— Criss Jami

3. The More You Know

The more you know, the more you realize you don't know. What is an area that interests you that you hope to learn more about in the future? Why?

"There is no human being from whom we cannot learn something if we are interested enough to dig deep."
— *Eleanor Roosevelt*

4. Learning from others
When was the last time you unexpectedly learned something new from a person you never would have thought to learn from?

"Fear doesn't shut you down; it wakes you up."
— Veronica Roth

5.The subtle whisper

My greatest fears have helped me to realize…

"Play around. Dive into absurdity and write. Take chances. You will succeed if you are fearless of failure."
— *Natalie Goldberg*

6. A simple life
Too much of anything could be bad for you. What do you need less of to feel happy?

"How you do anything is how you do everything."
— Hal Elrod

7. My actions show who I am

What might others learn from watching the way you do things?

"A brave man acknowledges the strength of others."
— *Veronica Roth*

8. Sincere appreciation

Name five of the strongest people you know and what qualities they
have that make you admire their strength.

"The more honest you are, the more open, the less fear you will have, because there's no anxiety about being exposed or revealed to others."
— Dalai Lama XIV

9. Opening Up

What is one thing about yourself that you are afraid other people will discover? If you can, take this week to share that hidden truth with at least one other person to see how you feel.

"It is hard to fail, but it is worse never to have tried to succeed."
— *Theodore Roosevelt*

10. A sudden realization

Failing isn't as scary as never doing....

"Every decision you make, makes you. Never let other people choose who you're going to be."
— *Cassandra Clare*

11. It All Works Out

What seemed like a bad decision at the time but has since turned into something great?

"Looking at beauty in the world, is the first step of purifying the mind."
— *Amit Ray*

12. Life will always find a way
I am calm because I can see the tranquility of the earth through…

"Have you noticed how many people who walk in the shade curse the Sun?"
— Idries Shah

13. Just tune in to it
Discuss the last time you were truly able to get lost in the moment.

"When we love, we always strive to become better than we are. When we strive to become better than we are, everything around us becomes better too."
— *Paulo Coelho*

14. Facing the Truth
I have to be honest with myself about...

"We are all hypocrites. We cannot see ourselves or judge ourselves the way we see and judge others."
— José Emilio Pacheco

15. Inner Dialogue

What are the things you judge other people on the most?

"Anyone can find the dirt in someone. Be the one that finds the gold."
— *Gaur Gopal Da*

16. Shining from Within
Pick out one or two of your flaws. How could someone else interpret these flaws as charming or endearing?

"Patience is a form of wisdom. It demonstrates that we understand and accept the fact that sometimes things must unfold in their own time."
— *Jon Kabat-Zinn*

17. Good things take time

What is the most valuable thing you learned from a time when patience was required?

"Fear, to a great extent, is born of a story we tell ourselves..."
— *Cheryl Strayed*

18. Fear or False Evidence Appearing Real

I have some irrational fears I know I can let go of such as...

"Live authentically. Why would you continue to compromise something that's beautiful to create something that is fake?"
— *Steve Maraboli*

19. Appreciating who I am

What are five things about you that are unique and five things about you that are just like everyone else?

"Your entire life changes the day that you decide you will no longer accept mediocrity for yourself."
— *Hal Elrod*

20. I Deserve More

You can easily identify fear like spiders, or failure. What's a fear you have that might be someone else's comfort?

"I do not ask the wounded person how he feels, I myself become the wounded person."
— Walt Whitman

21. What about them?

When was the last time you were able to feel the pain that somebody else was experiencing?

"Your true home is in the here and the now."
— *Thich Nhat Hanh*

22. Harmony of my heart

What do you ruminate over the most, and why do you think your mind obsesses over this aspect? How can you elicit positive change from these worries?

"Walk as if you are kissing the Earth with your feet."
— Thich Nhat Hanh

23.Relax and enjoy the ride

Go for a nature walk and find five beautiful things that you have never really appreciated. Why are they beautiful?

"Numbing the pain for a while will make it worse when you finally feel it."
— *J.K. Rowling*

24. Confronting My Feelings

When is the last time you ignored your negative emotions? Did this help them go away or make things worse?

"There is a huge amount of freedom that comes to you when you take nothing personally."
— *Don Miguel Ruiz*

25. Character traits
Criticism is hard to take sometimes, but I am able to accept it by…

"Mindfulness isn't difficult, we just need to remember to do it."
— *Sharon Salzberg*

26. Keeping Mindfulness in Our Days
The thoughts that keep me from being mindful are…

"An over-indulgence of anything, even something as pure as water, can intoxicate."
— Criss Jami

27. It happens!

I have been too obsessed with someone or something, and it caused me to be distracted from other important things in my life such as…

"I have never seen battles quite as terrifyingly beautiful as the ones I fight when my mind splinters and races, to swallow me into my own madness, again."
— *Nicole Lyons*

28. Totally at peace

I fight more battles inside myself than the fights I have outside in the rest of the world. What could make me feel more aligned?

"No matter what your age or your life path, whether making art is your career or your hobby or your dream, it is not too late or too egotistical or too selfish or too silly to work on your creativity."
— *Julia Cameron*

29. Never Too Late

I used to think it was "too late" to…

"How can a man know what is good or best for him, and yet chronically fail to act upon his knowledge?"
— Aristotle

30. Confronting Yourself

What are five things you know are bad for you, but you still do them anyway? What are five things that you know you should be doing, but you still choose to avoid?

"I find the best way to love someone is not to change them, but instead, help them reveal the greatest version of themselves."
— *Steve Maraboli*

31. We Flourish

Sometimes it can be hard to accept people for who they are. When was the last time you tried to change someone, and what did it take for you to accept them for who they are?

"I don't think you have time to waste not writing because you are afraid you won't be good at it."
— *Anne Lamott*

32. Life-force
Even when I judge myself, I can quiet these voices and keep moving forward because…

"We walk through so many myths of each other and ourselves; we are so thankful when someone sees us for who we are and accepts us."
— *Natalie Goldberg*

33. True nature

What value did you not realize you had until someone else pointed it out first? Have you been able to flourish this, or do you struggle still to see what they meant?

"The best way is not to fight it, just go. Don't be trying all the time to fix things. What you run from only stays with you longer. When you fight something, you only make it stronger."
— *Chuck Palahniuk*

34. Facing Reality
The last time I had an epiphany, I realized…

"We are only as strong as we are united, as weak as we are divided."
— *J.K. Rowling*

35. **Loved and loving**

Who do you turn to when you feel down? Why is this person your first choice?

"Don't complain about the snow on your neighbor's roof when your own doorstep is unclean." — *Confucius*

36. I Judge in others what I See in Myself
Sometimes I overlook my own flaws and instead point them out in others. Times that I have done this include....

"Nothing is more imminent than the impossible . . . what we must always foresee is the unforeseen."
— Victor Hugo

37. Inspiring Possibilities
Even absurd situations – like humans flying – seemed impossible. With the right perspective, they can be possible, like humans flying in airplanes. What seems impossible to you now but could be achievable if you shift your perspective?

"In essence, all of our words evoke, develop, and bring forth our reality. We always have the power to choose our words and our reality."
— *Julie Reisler*

38. The Ball is in your Court

As I think about my dreams, something amazing could happen now if I allow myself to…

"You're always you, and that don't change, and you're always changing, and there's nothing you can do about it."
— *Neil Gaiman,*

39. Holding the whole world

What has been the most life-changing moment in your existence?

"You own everything that happened to you. Tell your stories. If people wanted you to write warmly about them, they should have behaved better."
— Anne Lamott

40. Embracing Who I Am

Imagine you are your best friend giving a pitch to someone else about how great you are. What would they say?

"One must travel, to learn. Every day, now, old Scriptural phrases that never possessed any significance for me before, take to themselves a meaning."
— *Mark Twain*

41. Becoming more open and receptive

What place have you been that has taught you the most about yourself?

"The truth is not always beautiful, nor beautiful words the truth."
— Lao Tzu

42. Sometimes the best way out, is to go straight in

The hardest truth I've ever had to face is that….

"It's your life—but only if you make it so."
— Eleanor Roosevelt

43. Defining Myself

There are roadblocks and boundaries facing every person. Mine are...

"You can measure your worth by your dedication to your path, not by your successes or failures."
— *Elizabeth Gilbert*

44. Looking Forward
The things that keep me the most dedicated to my path are…

"The biggest adventure you can ever take is to live the life of your dreams."
— *Hal Elrod*

45. The life of my dreams

What is the scariest part about never achieving the life of your dreams?

"Creativity - like human life itself - begins in darkness"
— *Julia Cameron*

46. The Start of Something New

Sometimes adventures can start in a not so positive place. For example, maybe you had to move out of your home for a new job. What is an adventure you started that didn't have the happiest beginning but a much better ending?

"Others have seen what is and asked why. I have seen what could be and asked why not."
— *Pablo Picasso*

47. Uplifted and inspired

There are a few things I thought I could never do. These are…

"There are some choices you can only make once. You can't go back to where you made a choice and then take the other one."
— *Mary Hoffman*

48. The Right Choices

It can be easy to get stuck in our ways, but that can also keep us in a negative thinking space. When is the last time you chose to change your perspective, and what was the positive outcome from this?

"Write what disturbs you, what you fear, what you have not been willing to speak about. Be willing to be split open."
— *Natalie Goldberg*

49. Harmonious flow

What have you been putting off for too long that has been just too hard to accept? Reflect on this below and see if you can come to terms with…

"No one expected me. Everything awaited me."
— *Patti Smith*

50. How amazing I am!
My body is good at…. My mind is great at…. My soul is best at….

"There are moments when I wish I could roll back the clock and take all the sadness away, but I have the feeling that if I did, the joy would be gone as well."
— Nicholas Spark

51. Facing challenges

Sometimes we just have to take the bad with the good. What good do you have in your life, and what is the bad part that has to be accepted with this?

"The sun will shine on those who stand before it shines on those who kneel under them."
– African Proverb

52. I Stand Up for What I Believe

I am a good follower when I need to be, but even when someone else leads, I can show my authenticity by the way that I....

"I've got the key to my castle in the air, but whether I can unlock the door remains to be seen."
— Louisa May Alcott

53. Making things easier

What tools for life – whether they are there to fix a problem or provide knowledge – do you possess but fail to utilize?

"Are you proud of yourself tonight that you have insulted a total stranger whose circumstances you know nothing about?"
— *Harper Lee*

54. The things we miss

The last time I judged somebody too soon who was actually suffering, I found out that...

"True nobility isn't about being better than someone else. It's about being better than you used to be."
— Wayne W. Dyer

55. My Biggest Competition
It's time to stop competing with other people and instead know that you are your own biggest competitor. My biggest competitor's strengths are....

"Fear is a natural reaction to moving closer to the truth."
— *Pema Chodron*

56. Discomfort is good

What is the scariest thing about a new adventure?

"The first method for estimating the intelligence of a ruler is to look at the men he has around him."
— Niccolò Machiavelli

57. let's talk about friendship

Describe your three closest friends. What about them do you see in yourself?

"To understand the limitation of things, desire them."
— *Lao Tzu*

58. Roadblocks

What in your life makes you feel limited?

"Adventures do occur, but not punctually."
— *E.M. Forster*

59. Unexpected Surprises

The most shocking adventure I have ever been on was…

"All things of grace and beauty such that one holds them to one's heart have a common provenance in pain. Their birth in grief and ashes."
— *Cormac McCarthy*

60. Radiate beauty from the inside out

What beauty or grace do you have now because of the discomfort from pain you have experienced in the past?

"Pivoting is not the end of the disruption process, but the beginning of the next leg of your journey."
— Jay Samit

61. Backward thinking, forward action

In order to move fully onto the next chapter in my life, I need to let go of...

"There is always a gift in any challenge."
— *Bronnie Ware*

62. A precious gift

What struggle in your life provided you with the most valuable morsel of truth?

"To know others, know yourself first."
– Chinese Proverb

63. Feedback
What have you learned about yourself from other people?

"Maturity, one discovers, has everything to do with the acceptance of 'not knowing.'"
— *Mark Z. Danielewski*

64. I'm OK with Not Knowing

What is something you used to wish you desperately knew or understood but have since accepted that you might never know the truth?

"The emotion that can break your heart is sometimes the very one that heals it..."
— Nicholas Sparks

65. Recovering

There was a time in my life when my heart hurt so bad I thought it would never heal. Things got better, and eventually, I realized…

"We have to listen to understand in the same way we want to be understood."
— *Brené Brown*

66. Understanding Others

In the past, I have failed to see in others…

"There are no facts, only interpretations."
— *Friedrich Nietzsche*

67. Connecting to myself

Think of a time when you discovered a perspective that wasn't your own but one that someone else taught you. How did you notice this, and what did you do to change it in a positive way?

"I know not all that may be coming, but be it what it will, I'll go to it laughing."
— *Herman Melville*

68. Twist-Ending Adventures

What was something challenging at the time that you can laugh about now? Are you glad you lived through this experience?

"If I get to be me, I belong. If I have to be like you, I fit in."
— *Brené Brown*

69. Fitting In

You could make a puzzle piece fit where it doesn't belong by pressing it hard enough. What qualities about you are only present because they make you think you fit in?

"The things I carry are my thoughts. That's it. They are the only weight. My thoughts determine whether I am free and light or burdened."
— *Kamal Ravikant*

70. My challenges are my opportunities

I want to think more positive thoughts about…

"At the moment of vision, the eyes see nothing."
— William Golding

71. The mind's eye

What is something that you had seen many times but never really understood until you were older?

"Everything takes time. Bees have to move very fast to stay still."
— *David Foster Wallace*

72. True sense of worthiness

The most challenging thing about practicing, growing, and learning, aside from having patience, is…

"Don't let yesterday use up too much of today."
- Native American Proverb

73. Mind shift

Can you name a time when regret helped you learn something deeper about yourself?

"The questions are always more important than the answers."
— Randy Pausch

74. Questions

Five questions I hope to learn the answers to before I die are...

"What is real and what is not is for your heart to decide and for your heart to know."
— *Colleen Houck*

75. I Believe

What do you believe in that others do not? Not necessarily spiritual, but an idea like, "All people are good," or " Everything happens for a reason."

"If you wish to be good, first believe that you are bad."
— Epictetus

76. Embracing Imperfection

There have been times in my life when I questioned if I was a good person. I know that even questioning this means that I do have some good in me. The good and the bad show through the way that I...

"We can complain because rose bushes have thorns or rejoice because thorns have roses."
— Alphonse Karr

77. The Flip Side

Sometimes beauty is only found through pain. What painful experience has shown you something beautiful about life?

"Remember, there are beginnings in endings, through destruction there comes life."
— Nikita Gill

78. A world of new possibilities

Sometimes life might feel like it's ending, but that can really be the start of something great. When is the last time that something ended, and you discovered it was a chance at a new start?

"Failure is an event, it is not a person—yesterday ended last night—today is a brand-new day and it's yours."
— Zig Ziglar

79. The freedom you desire
I can be more comfortable with failure by…

"A born king is a very rare being."
— *Jean-Jacques Rousseau*

80. ...and everything changed.

We usually go through at least one enlightenment in our life where the person that we are shifts. What was this moment for you?

"Understanding is the first step to acceptance, and only with acceptance can there be recovery."
— *J.K. Rowling*

81. Peeling away the layers

What was the hardest truth about yourself you had to learn to accept?

"Kidding yourself doesn't require that you have a sense of humor. But a sense of humor comes in handy for almost everything else."
— *Carrie Fisher*

82. Making peace with yourself
The last time that I had to confront myself and stop pretending was when…

Self-discovery writing prompts:
Overflowing Self-Love

"Fortunate are those who take the first steps."
— *Paulo Coelho*

83. The gift of self-love
What would it take for you to truly love yourself?

"A heart filled with anger has no room for love."
— Joan Lunden

84. Disarm with charm

There have been times when I hated someone or something before I loved it. My perspective changed when…

"Great poetry, whether written in Greek or in English, needs no other interpreter than a responsive heart."
— Helen Keller

85. The eyes of love

Art that makes my heart smile is....

"Everyone who is successful must have dreamed of something."
- Native American Proverb

86. A Secret Dream

A dream that I don't share with others is that I secretly hope...

"Feeling too much is a hell of a lot better than feeling nothing."
— *Nora Roberts*

87. Follow your heart

Is it easier for you to shut out your emotions or to let yourself feel them fully? Why?

"You must never be fearful about what you are doing when it is right."

— *Rosa Parks*

88. Living a Happier Life

Something that felt wrong at first but now feels right is…

"Making a dream into reality begins with what you have, not with what you are waiting on."
— *T.F. Hodge*

89. Happy along the way
Sometimes the journey is more fulfilling than the end goal. The last time that I found abundance and excitement in the journey rather than the end goal was…

"If you can, serve other people, other sentient beings. If not, at least refrain from harming them. I think that is the whole basis of my philosophy."
— *Dalai Lama XIV*

90. Loving with empathy

How do you know if you are truly helping someone or if you could be unintentionally hurting them?

"It's the possibility of having a dream come true that makes life interesting."
— *Paulo Coelho*

91. My Dreams Fuel Me
If my dreams were to come true tomorrow, my life would look like…

"I don't think of all the misery, but of the beauty that still remains."
— Anne Frank

92. Silver Lining

The last time I was depressed or hopeless, I was able to pull myself
out of this mood by discovering the beauty of...

"It does not matter how long you are spending on the earth, how much money you have gathered or how much attention you have received. It is the amount of positive vibration you have radiated in life that matters."
— *Amit Ray*

93. Savoring the Moment
I make sure to live life to the fullest. I can soak up all the good vibrations of each and every moment by...

"Art has the power to render sorrow beautiful, make loneliness a shared experience, and transform despair into hope."
— *Brené Brown*

94. Make your heart sing

When was the last time you connected with someone because of art, whether it was because you both loved the same movie, song, or painting? Describe this experience.

"It's so hard to forget pain, but it's even harder to remember sweetness. We have no scar to show for happiness. We learn so little from peace."
— Chuck Palahniuk

95. A new perspective

Pain can stain our memories. What goodness have you forgotten because the pain from the same experience overshadowed the happiness?

"What you focus on expands."
– Oprah Winfrey

96. It Feels Good to Give

The best part about giving is....

"Take responsibility of your own happiness, never put it in other people's hands."
— *Roy T. Bennett*

97. The path to more joy

When was the last time you chose to be happy?

"Plant seeds of happiness, hope, success, and love; it will all come back to you in abundance. This is the law of nature."
— *Steve Maraboli*

98. Celebration!

What is something you've done in the past that ended up coming back to you and provided abundance later?

"You feel good not because the world is right, but your world is right because you feel good."
— Wayne W. Dye

99. Unexpected

As I'm thinking about my past relationships, at first I struggled with…. But then it got easier because…

"Life is a series of natural and spontaneous changes. Don't resist them; that only creates sorrow. Let reality be reality. Let things flow naturally forward in whatever way they like."
— Lao Tzu

100. Welcoming Spontaneity

The most unexpected thing I experienced, which I had to stop resisting was....

"How did one not obsess over something wonderful? How did one like something a reasonable amount?"
— *Helen Hoang*

101. Losing balance

What do you do to balance your emotional state between loving something or someone and being obsessed with that same thing? What is the biggest struggle of this balance for you?

"With mirth and laughter let old wrinkles come."
— *William Shakespeare*

102. The Joy of Growing

When is a time you remember laughing so hard you cried? What caused this?

"People are not disturbed by things, but by the views they take of them."

— Epictetus

103. The Beauty of Imperfection

When you're thinking about your biggest flaws, in what ways could these become attractive to someone?

"We must actively, consciously, consistently, and creatively nurture our artist selves."
— Julia Cameron

104. Happiness and creativity
What do you do to nurture your creativity?

"A storyteller makes up things to help other people; a liar makes up things to help himself."
— *Daniel Wallace*

105. Happiness and integrity

Who is your most honest friend, and what is it about them that makes you know you can trust them?

"Happiness then, is found to be something perfect and self-sufficient, being the end to which our actions are directed."
— Aristotle

106. Happiness is Natural

I do not have to wait for happiness to come into my life. I can find happiness now by...

"Be in your own skin, as an act of self-loving."
— *H. Raven Rose*

107. I can feel it
It feels so good to be myself because…

"When you really know somebody you can't hate them. Or maybe it's just that you can't really know them until you stop hating them."
— *Orson Scott Card*

108. Love and compromise

What is one thing someone you love does that drives you crazy? Describe why it's easy for you to love them.

"Leap, and the net will appear."
— Julia Cameron

109. Taking the Jump

Who helps you the most when you are going through something scary?

"Each of us is an artist of our days; the greater our integrity and awareness, the more original and creative our time will become."
— *John O'Donohue*

110. Art and self-love
Even if you can't draw, paint, sculpt, or do any other traditional "artistic" activities, what is it about you that makes you an artist?

"Be careful the stories you're telling yourself about your current circumstances; a head full of negative thoughts has no space for positive ones."
— Roy T. Bennett

111. Love is spontaneous

What is one thing that can instantly make you smile and why?

"If a man cannot understand the beauty of life, it is probably because life never understood the beauty in him."
— *Criss Jami*

112. A feeling that keeps building
I believe that life is beautiful because…

"Research has shown that we virtually become like the average of the five people we spend the most time with."
— *Hal Elrod*

113. Friends and exciting experiences
What does being a good friend mean to you?

"This is a good sign, having a broken heart. It means we have tried for something."
— *Elizabeth Gilbert*

114. Growing Perspectives

What do you only know now about positivity that you had to learn through age?

"Mirrors are perpetually deceitful. They lie and steal your true self.
They reveal only what your mind believes it sees."
— Dee Remy

115. Beyond the Mirror
What is seen in you that goes beyond your physical attributes?

"If you have a strong purpose in life, you don't have to be pushed.
Your passion will drive you there."
— Roy T. Bennett

116. Do what you love
Something positive that I always end up going back to is....

"Friendship ... is born at the moment when one man says to another 'What! You too? I thought that no one but myself . . .'"
— *C.S. Lewis*

117. Choosing your Family
What does family mean to you? What creates a good family?

"Nothing changes in your life without action."
— Hal Elrod

118. The Spark
What ignites your fire?

"I recognize that winning is not everything, but the effort to win is."
— Zig Ziglar

119. Playtime

A time when I lost but still enjoyed playing "the game" was...

"Listen, or your tongue will make you deaf."
- Native American Proverb

120. Cherishing Others

Who has been the most important person in your life? What do they expect from you and why?

"Love is a decision—not an emotion!"
— Lao Tzu

121. I Choose to Love
I have learned how to love by....

"Life is an echo. What you send out comes back. What you sow you reap. What you give you get. What you see in others exists in you."
— *Zig Ziglar*

122. Give to receive
One time when I sent something out in the world, I got it back when...

"You don't love someone because they're perfect, you love them in spite of the fact that they're not."
— *Jodi Picoult*

123. It's the little things that matters

What is the cutest, most charming, or most endearing flaw that someone you admire has? Do they realize this makes them unique?

"My point is, life is about balance. The good and the bad. The highs and the lows. The Pina and the colada."
— *Ellen DeGeneres*

124. Balancing Life

The biggest struggle I have with balance is…

"If life throws you a few bad notes or vibrations, don't let them interrupt or alter your song."
— Suzy Kassem

125. Positive momentum

What areas of your life makes you feel happy when others commonly struggle? What do you think makes you different from the rest in this sense?

"Friends are God's way of apologizing for your family."
— *Dr. Wayne W. Dyer*

126. Cultivate love

What is your best family memory, and why does it mean so much for you to this day?

"Love is like the wind, you can't see it but you can feel it."
— *Nicholas Sparks*

127. Unexpected Love

What is one thing you didn't expect about love? What feeling or common thought has surprised you in your relationships?

"Whatever happens around you, don't take it personally... Nothing other people do is because of you. It is because of themselves."
— *Don Miguel Ruiz*

128. Self-compassion

A time when my feelings were hurt but then I realized that this person didn't mean to harm me because…

"For most people, the fear of loss is much greater than the desire for gain."
— Anthony Robbins

129. A self-loving masterpiece

The things I have gained in this life that make me smile the most are…

"You can't stay in your corner of the Forest waiting for others to come to you. You have to go to them sometimes."
— A.A. Milne

130. Meeting New People

The last time I went out to make a friend, I was able to make this connection by...

"There is no greater agony than bearing an untold story inside you."
— *Maya Angelou*

131. I set myself free
I just want to shout from the rooftops that…

"Before you find your soul mate, you must first discover your soul."
— Charles F. Glassman

132. You deserve it
I am able to love other people because, through loving myself first, I have learned...

"Don't worry about trying to impress people. Just focus on how you can add value to their lives."
— Hal Elrod

133. Those Who Mind Don't Matter

What do others accept from you that someone else might not like? Why is it important for friends to be more open and embracing of our flaws?

"What should young people do with their lives today? Many things, obviously. But the most daring thing is to create stable communities in which the terrible disease of loneliness can be cured."
— *Kurt Vonnegut*

134. Happy and energized

You can sometimes still be lonely even in a crowded room. What helps you feel cheerful when you are alone or when you are with others?

"Don't be afraid of enemies who attack you. Be afraid of the friends who flatter you."
— Dale Carnegie

135. Changing your social circle

I have some people in my life I might need to work on cutting out in the future, and they don't fully appreciate me because...

"Remember that wherever your heart is, there you will find your treasure."
— *Paulo Coelho*

136. Unlimited abundance

What would your ideal treasure chest be filled with?

"I am the wisest man alive, for I know one thing, and that is that I know nothing."
— Plato

137. learning to love

What is something that you thought you knew about love but realized later you had a lot left to learn?

"Practice isn't the thing you do once you're good. It's the thing you do that makes you good."
— Malcolm Gladwell

138. Practice Makes Perfect
To feel more love in my life, I need to practice…

"And remember, no matter where you go, there you are."
— Confucius

139. Dating yourself

What do you enjoy most about being alone and spending time with yourself?

"Love is that micro-moment of warmth and connection that you share with another living being."
— *Barbara Fredrickson*

140. L-O-V-E
For me, Love is…

Self-discovery writing prompts: Elevating Self-Esteem

"We must do our work for its own sake, not for fortune or attention or applause."
— *Steven Pressfield*

141. Powerful Intention
What keeps you focused even when everything is seemingly falling apart?

"Never feel shame for trying and failing for he who has never failed is he who has never tried."
— *Og Mandino*

142. A radiant smile

My failures do not define me but instead display my growth. A failure I used to be ashamed of but am proud of now is…

"We all need to be seen and honored in the same way that we all need to breathe."
— *Brené Brown*

143. Feeling Appreciated

Who is someone you believe appreciates you fully, and what do they do to show this?

"With virtue you can't be completely poor; without it you can't be truly rich."
− Chinese Proverb

144. I am Rich

When you take money out of the equation, how else are you rich?

"The most fundamental aggression to ourselves, the most fundamental harm we can do to ourselves, is to remain ignorant by not having the courage and the respect to look at ourselves honestly and gently."
— Pema Chödrön

145. Looking Inward
I can show more of who I am on the inside by outwardly…

"The most valuable gift you can give yourself is the time to nurture the unique spirit that is you."
— *Oprah Winfrey*

146. Unshakable

What is a time that your hope pushed you through even when others doubted you?

"Your greatest self has been waiting your whole life; don't make it wait any longer."
— *Steve Maraboli*

147. Defying the architect of decay

What change have you pushed off for too long, and what do you plan to do to confront it and grow?

"Being yourself means being okay with your own desires. It means trusting the guidance you get from your heart."
— *Henri Junttila*

148. Remember who you are
I remind myself of who I am daily by...

"The thing I realize is, that it's not what you take, it's what you leave."
— Jennifer Niven

149. My Legacy
If there is one thing I could make sure other people thought of me, it would be...

"You don't always have to chop with the sword of truth. You can point with it too."
— *Anne Lamott*

150. Getting to the Truth

A time when I called out the truth for someone who wasn't ready to hear it was…

"Wealth should never be your goal in life. True wealth is of the heart, not of the purse."
— Og Mandino

151. Prosperity Mindset

I am already wealthy because…

"I am a part of all that I have met."
— Alfred Tennyson

152. Unfold your own story

Every experience we have ever been through is one that helps to define us. If you were to write your autobiography, what are the defining moments that helped create you as an individual?

"The greater intellect one has, the more originality one finds in men. Ordinary persons find no difference between men."
— *Blaise Pascal*

153. Stepping into your greatness

Who is the most unique person you know (besides yourself), and what sets them apart from the rest?

"I realized then that even though I was a tiny speck in an infinite cosmos, a blip on the timeline of eternity, I was not without purpose."
— *R.J. Anderson*

154. Your greatest self
I am small compared to the Earth, but I am mighty because...

"Being ourselves means sometimes having to find the courage to stand alone, totally alone."
— *Brené Brown*

155. Walk as if you are kissing the earth with your feet
The last time I stood up for something, even though I was standing alone, was when...

"There will never be another you. The planet desperately needs your unique purpose, passion and presence."
— *Julie Reisler*

156. Special
I have something special that no one else can say the same. This is...

"Persistence. Perfection. Patience. Power. Prioritize your passion. It keeps you sane."
— Criss Jami

157. Dreams to reality

I am able to be an independent person and achieve the things I want. I know when to ask for help when I need it, but I truly possess all the things required to achieve my dreams because I have…

"If we hope to go anywhere or develop ourselves in any way, we can only step from where we are standing. If we don't really know where we are standing... We may only go in circles..."
— Jon Kabat-Zinn

158. Starting anywhere is better than nowhere
What are your biggest reasons to change your life now?

"There's really no honor in proving that you can carry the entire load on your own shoulders. And...it's lonely."
— *Amanda Palmer*

159. Strength comes from vulnerability
Sometimes our strength is shown through the way that we are able to ask others for help. What is a moment when you tried to do it on your own but decided instead that you needed to seek help from someone else?

"Our job in this life is not to shape ourselves into some ideal we imagine we ought to be, but to find out who we already are and become it."
— *Steven Pressfield*

160. You are ready
The things that awaken the person I am inside are…

"The goal in life is not to attain some imaginary ideal; it is to find and fully use our own gifts."
— *Gay Hendricks*

161. A personal enjoyment
The greatest gifts I can offer this world are...

"There is no disgrace in honest failure; there is disgrace in fearing to fail."
— *Henry Ford*

162. Failing forward

I look forward to future moments when I learn from failure because it means....

"Whenever you become anxious or stressed, outer purpose has taken over, and you lost sight of your inner purpose. You have forgotten that your state of consciousness is primary, all else secondary."
— *Eckhart Tolle*

163. Clarity Through Purpose

My virtues, the morals that keep me grounded, are…

*"Don't be satisfied with stories, how things have gone with others.
Unfold your own myth."*
— Rumi

164. A sense of who you are
What opinion do you have that seems rare among people you know?

"Mental pain is less dramatic than physical pain, but it is more common and also [harder] to bear. The frequent attempt to conceal mental pain increases the burden: it is easier to say, 'My tooth is aching' than to say, 'My heart is broken'."
— *C.S. Lewis*

165. Asking for Help
How are you able to ask for help when you are hurting emotionally?

"You can't stop the waves, but you can learn to surf."
— *Jon Kabat-Zinn*

166. Just let it come naturally
What seemingly normal thing can you do with originality?

"Hope is a start. But hope needs action to win victories."
— David J. Schwartz

167. Serenity

What keeps you calm even when you're starting to get scared of failing or losing?

"Grace strengthens us. It strengthens our hearts, awakens in us the courage to stand firm."
— *Charles R. Swindoll*

168. A different approach

When did you last deliberately avoid something because you were simply embarrassed of what others would think of you? What can you do in the future to prevent this from happening again?

"And yet it takes only the smallest pleasure or pain to teach us time's malleability."
— Julian Barnes

169. The spice of life
The most exciting change I ever experienced was…

"No one who ever led a nation got there by following the path of another."
— Jay Samit

170. Make your life be your art
I march to the beat of my own drum by…

"Success is most often achieved by those who don't know that failure is inevitable."
— *Coco Chanel*

171. The workshop of your mind

I am not afraid to fail because I know it makes me a stronger person. The last time I failed, I was able to pick myself back up, and I learned a valuable lesson…

"Stay true to yourself. An original is worth more than a copy."
— *Suzy Kassem*

172. The courage to be yourself
Even when I am in a crowd of 1,000 people, I stand out because…

"The counterfeit innovator is wildly self-confident. The real one is scared to death."
— *Steven Pressfield*

173. The past is not today

My fears from my past no longer keep me from…

"Rather, it is bearing in mind what is most important to you so that it is not lost or betrayed in the heat and reactivity of a particular moment."
— *Jon Kabat-Zinn*

174. At the click of a finger

When is the last time you thought you were stuck in a situation but took the initiative and were able to elicit positive change?

"Originality is the best form of rebellion."
— *Mike Sasso*

175. Dare to Be Different
The most exciting thing about being different is...

"We realize the importance of our voices only when we are silenced."
— *Malala Yousafzai*

176. Being too cautious

The last time I had something to say but stayed quiet, I...

"If something comes up in your writing that is scary or naked, dive right into it. It probably has lots of energy."
— *Natalie Goldberg*

177. Vibrancy

What gives power to your courage?

"No one has ever become poor by giving."
— Anne Frank

178. An act of kindness

When was the last time you could have given but decided not to because you were worried about yourself?

"Scared is what you're feeling. Brave is what you're doing."
— Emma Donoghue

179. Stories we tell ourselves

When was the last time you were afraid to do something, but you didn't let that fear hold you down, and you ended up succeeding?

"A wind that blows aimlessly is no good to anyone."
— *Rick Riordan*

180. It feels good to be lost in the right direction
Even when I fall off track, I still know which direction to go because…

"Abundance arrives in the physical world when the inner world is ready to receive it. When we give ourselves permission to experience abundance, it always shows up."
— *Pam Malow-Isham*

181. What will you not miss until it's gone?

Sometimes we don't see our wealth even when it's staring right at us. When is the last time you took something for granted that you ended up not being able to get back?

"Don't look at your feet to see if you are doing it right. Just dance."
— *Anne Lamott*

182. I Am Free
The last time I let loose without being embarrassed or scared of judgement was when…

"Until we can receive with an open heart, we're never really giving with an open heart. When we attach judgment to receiving help, we knowingly or unknowingly attach judgment to giving help."
— Brené Brown

183. Making a choice

Would you still give if no one was ever allowed to know of your generosity? Be honest and describe why you would or would not.

"Incredible change happens in your life when you decide to take control of what you do have power over instead of craving control over what you don't."
— Steve Maraboli

184. Find your inner strength

Name a moment when you weren't able to change anything about the situation but still gained power by controlling your emotions and your response. What was it that gave you power to do this?

"Sometimes people let the same problem make them miserable for years when they could just say, 'So what.' That's one of my favorite things to say. So what."
— Andy Warhol

185. Who Cares?
The last time I said, "So what?" I…

"Worry never robs tomorrow of its sorrow, it only saps today of its joy."
— Gaur Gopal Das

186. Thinking of opportunity instead of security

Sometimes life is going to be uncomfortable no matter how much we might try to avoid that. What is one thing that used to make you uncomfortable that you are content with now?

"Learn to light a candle in the darkest moments of someone's life. Be the light that helps others see; it is what gives life its deepest significance."
— *Roy T. Bennett*

187. Help others find their way

When was the last time you stepped up when someone else really needed you? What happened?

"The future will present insurmountable problems- only when we consider them insurmountable."
— *Thomas S. Monson*

188. Victory

The most surprised I have ever been with myself for overcoming a challenge was when...

"Life is either a daring adventure or nothing at all."
— *Helen Keller*

189. My Challenging Obstacles

What is the most daring thing you have done within the past year since starting this journal?

"It's not always necessary to be strong, but to feel strong."
— *Jon Krakauer*

190. When love requires courage

What does true bravery look like to you?

"Life has no remote....get up and change it yourself!"
— Mark A. Cooper

191. A decisive moment

When is the last time you chose to change your life, and what was the catalyst that made this happen?

"No one can make you feel inferior without your consent."
— *Eleanor Roosevelt*

192. it doesn't matter what they think
When was the last time somebody hurt your feelings and you chose not to let this bother you? If you haven't been able to think of this moment, then reflect on what the challenges are with overcoming other people's definitions of you.

"If you are not afraid of the voices inside you, you will not fear the critics outside you."
— *Natalie Goldberg*

193. Share your courage with others

There have been moments when I was afraid to speak my mind. I got over this fear, and I'm able to use my voice because…

"It's not whether you get knocked down, it's whether you get up."
— *Vince Lombardi*

194. You're capable of more than you know

When was the last time you failed and then decided to try again? What was it that helped give you strength to keep pushing forward?

"Without being push to the wall, we will have remained in our comfortable zone. But this circumstance challenges us to find the courage to move on."
— *Lailah Gifty Akita*

195. Life is changing, better keep moving
The last time I was pushed past my boundaries was when...

"Let others determine your worth and you're already lost, because no one wants people worth more than themselves."
— *Peter V. Brett*

196. My Values

What are five valuable characteristics about yourself that other people have found in you? Do you see the same values? What are five values that you believe other people don't always see in you?

"If you're reading this...Congratulations, you're alive.
If that's not something to smile about, then I don't know what is."
— Chad Sugg

197. Happiness and meaning
We spend life looking for answers but often forget the answer
already exists inside of us. My purpose is...

"There never was a moment, and never will be, when we are without the power to alter our destiny."
— *Steven Pressfield*

198. Keep the vision in mind

I am destined to…

"It is our duty to select the best and most dependable theory that human intelligence can supply and use it as a raft to ride the seas of life."
— Plato

199. Self-empowered
I have faith in my abilities because...

"If I have learned anything in this long life of mine, it is this: in love we find out who we want to be; in war we find out who we are."
— *Kristin Hannah*

200. The start of something new

My biggest inspiration for who I want to be is... My biggest inspiration for who I DON'T want to be is...

"The man who moves a mountain begins by carrying away small stones."
— Confucius

201. A New Beginning

My journey is not over just yet. This is merely a chapter in a long book of life. I am ready to start....

Conclusion

There is nothing more fulfilling than completing a task you set out to do. Not everyone will be able to make it to the end, whether it is because they struggle with facing some of their deepest darkest thoughts or because they have challenges sticking to a schedule.

The importance of this book was to help you discover who you truly are. We know what we like, what experiences we have, and what labels we've given ourselves and received from others. Unfortunately, not everyone will be able to meet who they are deep down.

You went through everything from self-awareness to self-love and self-esteem. The most important factor of all was you! It was not an easy journey, but you should be endlessly proud of the things you have done to get to know yourself.

The most important thing to take away from this book is that you are able to do it on your own. I provided some guidance, but in reality, it was you who put in the hard work. It was your ideas and creative juices that allowed you to become the person you are today. Every experience you have had and everything you've done in this life has led you to where you are now.

You've met yourself, but the journey doesn't stop there. You will be the only constant throughout this life. Some people will be in and out of your life, intentionally or accidentally, but it will always be you that is still there at the end of the day. Nurture and grow your relationship to find the most fulfillment possible in this life.

About the Author

Calista McBride is a writer, author and former middle school teacher. She's now dedicated to help people gain the confidence to take action and start a journey towards living a fulfilled and meaningful life. Calista leverages the art and science of success, high-performance practices and self-mastery to produce uplifting and transformative material.

Her mission is to inspire you, to think bigger.

Thank you

We've come to the end of this Journal. I just want to say thank you for reading.

If you enjoyed it, I'd be grateful if you left a review on Amazon.

It'll take a few seconds and it'll mean the world to me because as an independent author every single review counts. Even a short review is enough.

Thank you very much for your kind support!

I also would love hear about your ideas, tips and questions. let me know at calistamcbride@gmail.com

With Love,

Calista

References

Akita, L. (2015). On Eagles Wings: Rise. (n.p.)

Albom, M. (2009). Have a little faith: A true story.

Alcott, L. M. (2004). Little women. New York: Signet Classic.

Amish, & Tripathi, A. (2012). The Secrets of the Nagas: Shiva Trilogy 2. Chennai: Westland Books Pvt. Ltd.

Anderson, R. (2011). Ultraviolet. Orchard.

Angelou, M. (2009). I know why the caged bird sings. New York: Random House Trade Paperbacks.

Aristotle., Bartlett, R. C., & Collins, S. D. (2011). Aristotle's Nicomachean ethics. Chicago: University of Chicago Press.

Atwood, M. (2009). The year of the flood: A novel. Toronto: McClelland & Stewart.

Baldwin, J. (1963). The fire next time. New York: Dial Press.

Barnes, J. (2011). The Sens of an Ending. Jonathan Cape.

Bennett, R. (2016). The Light in the Heart. Roy Bennett.

Bonhoeffer, D., Gremmels, C., Bethge, E., Bethge, R., Tödt, I., & De, G. J. W. (2010). Letters and papers from prison. Minneapolis, Minn: Fortress Press.

Bourdain, A. (2007). Kitchen confidential: adventures in the culinary underbelly. Updated edition [New York]: Harper Perennial.

Branson, R., & Mulraney, A. (2010). Screw it, let's do it. Tullamarine, Vic: Bolinda Audio.

Brett, P. (2009). The Warded Man. Random House.

Briggs, P. (2002). Dragon Bones. Ace Fantasy.

Brink, C. R., & Seredy, K. (1935). Caddie Woodlawn. New York: Macmillan Co.

Brink, C. R., & Seredy, K. (1935). Caddie Woodlawn. New York: Macmillan Co.

Brown, B. (2017). Braving the wilderness: The quest for true belonging and the courage to stand alone. New York: Random House.

Brown, B., & OverDrive Inc. (2010). The gifts of imperfection: Let go of who you think you're supposed to be and embrace who you are. Center City, MN: Hazelden.

Brown, D. (2016). Inferno: A novel.

Brown, L. (1994). Live Your Dreams. William Morrow Paperbacks.

Bstan-'dzin-rgya-mtsho, Dalai Lama XIV, 1935-. (1998). The art of happiness : a handbook for living. New York :Riverhead Books,

Burney, F., & Howard, S. K. (2000). Evelina, or, A young lady's entrance into the world: In a series of letters. Peterborough, Ont: Broadview Press.

Cameron, J. (2002). The artist's way: A spiritual path to higher creativity. New York: J.P. Tarcher/Putnam.

Camus, A. (1965). The myth of Sisyphus, and other essays. London: H. Hamilton.

Camus, A., Gilbert, S., & O'Brien, J. (2004). The plague: The fall ; Exile and the kingdom ; and, selected essays. New York: Everyman's Library.

Camus, A., Thody, P., & O'Brien, J. (1998). Notebooks, 1935-1951. New York: Marlowe & Co.

Card, O. S., & Harris, J. (1986). Speaker for the dead. New York, N.Y: TOR.

Carnegie, Dale, 1888-1955. (2009). How to win friends and influence people. New York :Simon & Schuster

Chesterton, G. K. (1959). Orthodoxy. Garden City, N.Y: Image Books.

Chopra, D. (2009). Reinventing the Body, Resurrecting the Soul: How to Create a New You. Harmony.

Chödrön, P. (2000). When things fall apart: Heart advice for difficult times. Boston: Shambhala.

Clare, C., Wasserman, R., Falahee, J. (2015). The Lost Herondale. (n.p.)

Coelho, P. (1998). The alchemist. San Francisco: HarperSanFrancisco.

Coelho, P. (2006). By the River Piedra I Sat Down and Wept. HarperOne.

Coelho, P. (1998). The alchemist. San Francisco: HarperSanFrancisco.

Confucius, ., & In Waley, A. (1938). The Analects of Confucius. New York: Random House.

Cooper, J. E. (2013). Keeping a Journal: A Path to Uncovering Identity (and Keeping Your Sanity). Educational Perspectives, 46, 40-43.

Cooper, M. (2011). Operation Einstein. Infinity.

Corneille, P., Wilbur, R., & Corneille, P. (2009). Le Cid ; and, the liar. Boston: Mariner Books/Houghton Mifflin Harcourt.

Danielewski, M. Z., Zampanò, ., & In Truant, J. (2000). Mark Z. Danielewski's House of leaves.

Dante Alighieri, & Ciardi, J. (2001). The inferno. New York: Signet Classic.

Darwin, Charles, 1809-1882. (1859). On the origin of species by means of natural selection, or preservation of favoured races in the struggle for life. London :John Murray,

Das, G. G. (2018). Life's Amazing Secrets: How to Find Balance and Purpose in Your Life. Penguin Ananda.

Dawson, G. & Glaubman, R. (2001). Life is So Good. Penguin Books.

DeGeneres, E. (2013). Seriously--I'm kidding. Philadelphia: Running Press.

DeLiso, T. (2000). Legacy: The Power Within. Writers Club Press

Delosa, J. (2016). The ritual used by some of the world's leaders including Oprah and Richard Branson. Retrieved from https://www.smartcompany.com.au/entrepreneurs/ritual-used-worlds-leaders-including-oprah-richard-branson/

Descartes, René, 1596-1650. (1993). Discourse on method ; and, Meditations on first philosophy. Indianapolis :Hackett Pub. Co.

Dickens, C., & Schama, S. (1990). A tale of two cities. New York: Vintage Books.

Dickens, C., Browne, H. K., & Slater, M. (1978). Nicholas Nickleby. Harmondsworth: Penguin.

Dickens, C., Law, G., & Pinnington, A. J. (1998). Great expectations. Peterborough, Ont: Broadview Press.

Donoghue, E. (2010). Room: A novel. Toronto: HarperCollins.

Dowden, A. R., Warren, J. M., & Kambui, H. (2014). Three tiered model toward improved self-awareness and self-care. Ideas and research you can use: VISTAS.

Duhigg, Charles. (2012) The power of habit :why we do what we do in life and business New York : Random House

Dweck, Carol S.. (2008) Mindset :the new psychology of success New York : Ballantine Books

Dyer, J. (2018). Empath and The Highly Sensitive. (n.p.)

Dyer, W. W. (2004). The power of intention: Learning to co-create your world your way. Carlsbad, CA: Hay House.

Eisen, A. (1992). Believing in Ourselves: The Wisdom of Women. Ariel Books.

Elrod, H. (2014). The miracle morning: The not-so-obvious secret guaranteed to transform your life before 8AM.

Emerson, R. W., & In Emerson, E. W. (1903). The complete works of Ralph Waldo Emerson. Boston: Houghton, Mifflin and Co.

Epictetus, ., & Lebell, S. (2007). The art of living: The classic manual on virtue, happiness, and effectiveness. New York: HarperOne.

Fey, T. (2011). Bossypants. New York: Little, Brown.

Fisher, C. (2016). The princess diarist.

Ford, H., & Crowther, S. (1922). My life and work. Garden City, N.Y: Doubleday, Page & Co.

Forster, E. M., & Stallybrass, O. (1985). A passage to India. Harmondsworth: Penguin.

Francis, D. (1997). 10 lb Penalty. G.P. Putnam's Sons.

Frank, A. (1993). Anne Frank: The diary of a young girl. New York ; Toronto: Bantam Books.

Fredrickson, B. (2013). Love 2.0: How Our Supreme Emotion Affects Everything We Feel, Think, Do, and Become. Avery.

Fritson, K. K. (2008). Impact of Journaling on Students' Self-Efficacy and Locus of Control. InSight: A Journal of Scholarly Teaching, 3, 75-83.

Gandhi., & Gandhi, M. (19581969). All men are brothers: life and thoughts of Mohatma Gandhi as told in his own words.. Centennial reprint, 1869-1969. [New York]: Columbia University Press.

Gibran, K. 1., & Gibran, K. (2011). Kahlil Gibran's The prophet: And The art of peace (New illustrated ed.). London: Watkins.

Gibran, K. 1., & Gibran, K. (2011). Kahlil Gibran's The prophet: And The art of peace (New illustrated ed.). London: Watkins.

Gilbert, E. (2007). Eat, pray, love: One woman's search for everything across Italy, India, and Indonesia. New York: Penguin.

Gilbert, E. (2015). Big magic: Creative living beyond fear.

Gill, N. (2016). Your Soul is a River. Thought Catalog Books.

Gladwell, Malcolm. (2011) Outliers :the story of success New York : Back Bay Books

Glassman, C. (2009). Brain Drain The Breakthrough That Will Change Your Life. RTS Publishing.

Goldberg, Natalie. (1986). Writing down the bones : freeing the writer within. Boston : [New York] :Shambhala ; Distributed by Random House

Goodkind, T. (1994). Wizard's first rule.

Greene, G., In Lewis, R. W. B., & In Conn, P. J. (1970). The power and the glory. New York: Viking Press.

Greene, R., & Elffers, J. (2000). The 48 laws of power.

Hale, M. (2013). The Single Woman: Life, Love, and a Dash of Sass. Thomas Nelson.

Hamilton, Laurell K. (©2006) Mistral's kiss :a novel New York : Ballantine Books,

Han, J. (2014). To all the boys I've loved before. New York: Simon & Schuster BFYR.

Hanh, T. N. (2011). Your True Home: The Everyday Wisdom of Thich Nhat Hanh: 365 days of practical, powerful teachings from the beloved Zen teacher. Shambhala.

Hannah, K. (2015). The nightingale (First Edition.). New York, N.Y.: St. Martin's Press.

Hardy, B. (n.d.). Writing In A Journal Has Helped Me Create My Future And Achieve My Goals. Retrieved from https://www.inc.com/benjamin-p-hardy/how-i-use-my-journal-to-create-my-future-achieve-my-goals.html

Harris, M. (2005). Is journaling empowering? Students' perceptions of their reflective writing experience. Health SA Gesondheid, 10(2), 47-60.

Heath, C., & Heath, D. (2011). Switch: How to change things when change is hard. Waterville, Me: Thorndike Press.

Heinlein, Robert A. (Robert Anson), 1907-1988. (1991). Stranger in a strange land. New York :Ace Books,

Hendricks, G. (2009). The Big Leap: Conqure Your Hidden Fear and Take Life to the Next Level. HarperOne.

Hoang, H. (2018). The kiss quotient.

Hodge, T.F. (2009). From Within I Rise: Spiritual Triumph Over Death and Conscious encounters with "The Divine presence." America Star Books.

Hoffman, M. (2006). City of Flowers. Bloomsbury.

Houck, C., Boras, A., Jhaveri, S., & Brilliance Audio (Firm). (2011). Tiger's curse.

Hugo, V., Wilbour, C. E., & Bénichou, P. (1964). Les Miserables. New York: Washington Square Press.

Iansiti, M., Lakhani, K. R., McBrien, K., & Moon, M. (2017). Managing our hub economy: Strategy, ethics, and network competition in the age of digital superpower. Harvard Business Review, 95(5), 84-92.

Jalāl al-Dīn Rūmī., & Barks, C. (1996). The essential Rumi. 1st HarperCollins paperback ed. San Francisco, CA: Harper.

Jami, C. (2011). Salome: In Every Inch In Every Mile. CreateSpace.

Jefferson, T., In Boyd, J. P., In Bryan, M. R., In Butterfield, L. H., In Cullen, C. T., In Catanzariti, J., In Oberg, B., ... In McClure, J. P. (1950). The papers of Thomas Jefferson.

Junttila, H. (2013). Follow Your Heart: 21 Days to a Happier, More Fulfilling Life. (n.p.)

Kabat-Zinn, J. (1994). Wherever you go, there you are: Mindfulness meditation in everyday life. New York: Hyperion.

Kabat-Zinn, Jon. (2013). Full catastrophe living : using the wisdom of your body and mind to face stress, pain, and illness. New York :Bantam Books,

Kaling, M. (2011). Is everyone hanging out without me? (and other concerns). New York: Crown Archetype.

Karr, A. (2008). A Tour Round My Garden. Kessinger Publishing.

Kassem, S., & In Grim, R. (2011). Rise up and salute the sun: The writings of Suzy Kassem.

Keller, H., & Sullivan, A. (1954). The story of my life.

Kierkegaard, Søren, 1813-1855. (1980). The concept of anxiety : a simple psychologically orienting deliberation on the dogmatic issue of hereditary sin. Princeton, N.J. :Princeton University Press

King, F. B., & LaRocco, D. (2006). E-journaling: A strategy to support student reflection and understanding. Current Issues in Education, 9.

King, Martin Luther, Jr., 1929-1968. (1991). A testament of hope : the essential writings of Martin Luther King, Jr. San Francisco :HarperSanFrancisco

Kingsolver, Barbara. (1999, c1998) The poisonwood Bible :a novel New York : HarperPerennial

Krakauer, Jon. (1997). Into the wild. New York :Anchor Books,

Kreider, T. (2012). We Learn Nothing. Free Press.

L'Engle, M. (1965). The arm of the starfish. New York: Ariel Books.

Lamott, A. (1995). Bird by bird: some instructions on writing and life. 1st Anchor books edition. New York: Anchor Books.

Lamott, A. (2000). Traveling mercies: Some thoughts on faith.

Laozi. (1972). Tao te ching. New York :Vintage Books,

Lee, Harper. (2006). To kill a mockingbird. New York :Harper Perennial Modern Classics

Lessing, Doris, 1919-2013. (1962). The golden notebook. New York :Simon and Schuster

Lewis, C. S. (1960). The four loves.

219

Lewis, C. S. (1962). The problem of pain. New York: Macmillan.

Lewis, S. (1970). It can't happen here. New York: New American Library.

Lokos, A. (2010). Pocket Peace: Effective Practices for Enlightened Living. Tarcherperigee.

Lombardi, V & Heinz, W.C. (1963). Run to Daylight! Prentice Hall.

Lowry, Lois. (2002, c1993) The giver /New York : Laurel Leaf Books

Lunden, J. (2001). Wake-Up Calls: Making The Most Out of Every Day (Regardless of What Life Throws At You). McGraw-Hill.

Lyons, N. (2017). Hush. Feminine Collective Inc.

Maas, S. (2015). A Court of Thorns and Roses. Bloomsbury USA Childrens.

Machiavelli, N., Skinner, Q., & Price, R. (1988). The prince. Cambridge: Cambridge University Press.

Mandino, O. (1989). The greatest salesman in the world: Featuring the ten vows of success. New York, N.Y.: Bantam.

Maraboli, S. (2009). Life, the Truth, and Being Free. Better Today Publishing.

Marcus Aurelius, Emperor of Rome, 121-180. (1942). The meditations of Marcus Aurelius. Mount Vernon [N.Y.] :Peter Pauper Press,

McCarthy, C. (2006). The road. New York: Vintage Books.

McElhaney, N. (2017). Drowning Ophelia & Other Poetic Tragedies. Amazon.

McGill, B. (2012). Voice of Reason. Paper Lyon Publishing.

McGuire, S. (2017). Down Among the Sticks and Bones. Tor.com

Melville, Herman. Moby-Dick: Or, the Whale. Penguin Books, 2001. ... New York: Penguin Books, 2001.

Miller, A. (1991). The Ride Down Mt. Morgan. Penguin Books.

Milne, A. A. (Alan Alexander), 1882-1956. (2003). Winnie-the-Pooh. [New York] :Harper Children's Audio

Monson, T. (n.d.) Pathways To Perfection: Discourses of Thomas S. Monson. Shadow Mountain.

Montaigne, M. ., Cotton, C., & In Hazlitt, W. C. (1877). The essays of Montaigne. London: Reeves and Turner.

Muir, Kenneth. (1987). William Shakespeare, Antony and Cleopatra. Harmondsworth, Middlesex :Penguin Books

Murdoch, I. Nussbaum, M. (1973). The Black Prince. Penguin Classics.

Murnahan, B. (2010). Stress and Anxiety Reduction Due to Writing Diaries, Journals, E-mail, and Weblogs.

Naskar, A. (2019). All For Acceptance. (n.p.)

Nhất, H., & Kotler, A. (1991). Peace is every step: The path of mindfulness in everyday life. New York, N.Y: Bantam Books.

Niven, J. (2015). All the bright places (First edition.). New York: Alfred A. Knopf.

Oliver, L. (2011). Delirium. New York: Harper.

O'Donohue, J. (2008). To Bless the Space Between Us: A Book of Blessings.

Pacheco, J. (1987). Battles in the Desert Other Stories. New Directions.

Palahniuk, C. (2003). Diary: A novel. New York: Doubleday.

Palahniuk, C. (2012). Invisible monsters remix ([New ed.].). New York: W. W. Norton.

Palmer, A. (2014). The Art of Askin; or, How I Learned to Stop Worrying and Let People Help. Grand Central Publishing.

Parks, R., & Haskins, J. (1992). Rosa Parks: My story.

Pascal, Blaise, 1623-1662. (1958). Pascal's Pensées. New York :E.P. Dutton

Pausch, R. & Zaslow, J. (2008). The Last Lecture. Hyperion: New York.

Perkins, A. (2011). Anna and the French Kiss. Speak.

Picasso, P. (2000). Pablo Picasso: Metamorphoses of the Human Form: Graphic Works, 1895 – 1972. Prestel.

Picoult, Jodi, 1966-. (2005). My sister's keeper : a novel. New York :Washington Square Press.

Picoult, J. (2007). Nineteen minutes: A novel (1st Atria Books hardcover ed.). New York: Atria Books.

Plato. (1943). Plato's The Republic. New York :Books, Inc.

Pressfield, S. (2012). The war of art: Break through the blocks and win your inner creative battles.

Rath, T. (2015). Are You Fully Charged? The 3 Keys to Energizing Your Work and Life. Silicon Guild.

Ravikant, K. (2013). Live Your Truth. Self-Published.

Ray, A. (2015). Meditation: Insights and Inspirations. Inner Light Publishers.

Reisler, J. (2017). Get a PhD in YOU. A Course in Miraculous Self-Discovery. Empowered Living, LLC Books.

Remy, D. (2012). There Once Was a Boy. Brighton Publishing LLC.

Riordan, R. (2014). The blood of Olympus. New York: Hyperion.

Robbins, A. (1992). Awaken the giant within: How to take immediate control of your mental, emotional, physical & financial destiny!. New York: Simon & Schuster.

Roberts, N. (2006). Midnight Bayou. Jove.

Robinson, K., & Aronica, L. (2009). The element: How finding your passion changes everything. New York: Penguin Group USA.

Roosevelt, E. (1939). This is My Story. Garden City Publishing Co.

Roosevelt, E. (1960). You learn by living. New York: Harper.

Roosevelt, T., & Thomsen, B. (2003). The man in the arena: The selected writings of Theodore Roosevelt ; a reader. New York: Forge.

Rose, H. R. (2012). Shadow Selves: Double Happiness. eXu Publsihing.

Roth, V. (2012). Divergent. Rev. paperback edition. New York, NY: Katherine Tegen Books, an imprint of HarperCollins Publishers.

Rousseau, J.-J., & In Frankel, C. (1947). The social contract. New York: Hafner Pub. Co.

Rowling, J. K., author. (2002). Harry Potter and the goblet of fire. New York :Scholastic

Ruiz, M., & Mills, J. (1997). The four agreements: A practical guide to personal freedom.

Salvatore, R.A. (1990). Exile. Wizards of the Coast.

Salzberg, S. (2011). Real happiness: The power of meditation : a 28-day program. New York: Workman Pub.

Samit, J. (2015). Disrupt You! Master Personal Transformation, Seize Opportunity, and Thrive in the Era of Endless Innovation. Flatiron Books.

Saramago, J., & Pontiero, G. (2005). Blindness. London: Vintage Books.

Sasso, M. (2011). Being Human: Everything you Didn't Want to Know About Life. The Old Man Walking Publishing.

Schwartz, D. J. (2007). The magic of thinking big (1st Fireside ed.). New York: Simon & Schuster.

Schwarzenegger, A., Ticotin, R., Verhoeven, P., Feitshans, B., Shusett, R., O'Bannon, D., Stone, S., ... Carolco Home Video (Firm). (1990). Total recall. Van Nuys, CA: Carolco Home Video.

Seneca, L. A., & Campbell, R. (1969). Letters from a Stoic: Epistulae morales ad Lucilium. Harmondsworth: Penguin.

Shah, I. (1972). Reflections. Octagon Press, Limited.

Shakespeare, William, 1564-1616. The Merchant of Venice. Harlow, Essex, England :Longman, 1994.

Sharma, R. S. (1998). The monk who sold his Ferrari: A spiritual fable about fulfilling your dreams and reaching your destiny. Toronto: HarperCollins.

Smith, P. (2010). Just kids.

Solgot, H. (2005). Journaling for Personal and Professional Growth: Reflections of a Recent Student Teacher. Language Arts Journal of Michigan, 21(1), 13.

Sophocles, & Roche, P. (2004). The Oedipus plays of Sophocles: Oedipus the king, Oedipus at Colonos, Antigone. New York: Plume.

Sparks, N. (2006). At First Sight. Grand Central Publishing.

Sparks, N. (2007). A walk to remember. Unabridged. Westminster, Md.: Books on Tape.

Stanford Business. (2012). WrittenThe Value of "Values Affirmation." Retrieved from https://www.gsb.stanford.edu/insights/value-values-affirmation

Stevenson, R. L. (1972). The Silverado squatters: With an introduction by Oscar Lewis. Ashland [Ore.: Lewis Osborne.

Strayed, C. (2012). Wild: From lost to found on the Pacific Crest Trail. New York: Alfred A. Knopf.

Sugg, C. (2015). Monsters Under Your Head. CWS Press.

Swindoll, C. R. (1990). The grace awakening. Dallas: Word Pub..

Taylor, E. (1994). A Wreath of Roses. Virago.

Tennyson, A. T., & James R. Osgood and Company,. (1875). The complete poetical works of Alfred Tennyson.

Tolle, E. (2004). The power of now: A guide to spiritual enlightenment.

Tolle, E. (2005). A new earth: Awakening to your life's purpose. New York, N.Y: Dutton/Penguin Group.

Tracy, B. (1995). Maximum Achievement: Strategies and Skills that Will Unlock Your Hidden Powers to Succeed. Simon Schuster.

Twain, Mark, 1835-1910. The Innocents Abroad ; Roughing It. New York, N.Y. :Library of America : Distributed to the trade in the U.S. and Canada by the Viking Press, 1984.

Van, D. W. (2001). Flipped. New York: Knopf.

Vonnegut, K. (1999). Mother night. New York: Delta Trade Paperbacks.

Vonnegut, K. (1981). Palm Sunday: An autobiographical collage. New York: Delacorte Press.

Wallace, D. (2013). The Kings and Queens of Roam. Gallery Books.

Wallace, D. F. (1999). Brief interviews with hideous men. Boston: Little, Brown.

Ware, B. (2012). The top five regrets of the dying: A life transformed by the dearly departing. Carlsbad, Calif.: Hay House.

Warhol, A. (1975). The philosophy of Andy Warhol: From A to B and back again.

Whitman, W. (1921). Song of myself by Walt Whitman.

Wilson, D. (2015). Skyshaker. Dioscuri Press.

Woolf, V., DiBattista, M., & Hussey, M. (2006). Orlando: A biography. Orlando, Fla: Harcourt.

Yousafzai, M., & Lamb, C. (2013). I am Malala: The girl who stood up for education and was shot by the Taliban (First edition.). New York: Little, Brown and Company.

Zeus, W. (2010). Sun Beyond the Clouds. Createspace Independent Publishing Platform.

Ziglar, Z. (1974). See You at the Top. Pelican Publishing Company.

Ōe, K. (1996). Hiroshima Notes. Grove Press.

Made in the USA
Monee, IL
24 April 2020